Best
Car

IMAGES OF ENGLAND

WASHINGTON

IMAGES OF ENGLAND

WASHINGTON

CAROL ROBERTON

TEMPUS

Frontispiece: Children on a winter's day at Washington Wetlands Centre in the late 1970s.

First published 2006

Tempus Publishing Limited
The Mill, Brimscombe Port,
Stroud, Gloucestershire, GL5 2QG
www.tempus-publishing.com

British Library Cataloguing in Publication Data.
A catalogue record for this book is available from the British Library.

ISBN 0 7524 4000 4

Typesetting and origination by Tempus Publishing Limited.
Printed in Great Britain.

Contents

Acknowledgements

This book owes everything to the knowledge, help and support of a number of organisatons and individuals who have contributed pictures and information. The majority of the pictures come from the archives of Washington Town Centre Library and Sunderland City Library, Beamish Open Air Museum, Washington parish church of Holy Trinity, the National Trust at Washington Old Hall, Washington Arts Centre, and Washington Wildfowl and Wetlands Centre; thanks are due to the helpful staff at all of these organisations. A special debt is owed to David Young for contributions from his private collection and for sharing his knowledge of local history. Special thanks are also due to the following individuals for pictures, information and friendship given in the course of researching this book: Anne Forth, Jim Lawson, Elaine Naylor, John Wood, Ashley Sutherland, Phil Hall, James Smith, Bill Craddock, Kate Gardner, Chris Francis, Leanne McCormella.

Useful background information was found in the following reference material: Margot Johnson, *Washington Church*; Ashley Sutherland and John Wood, *Washington Then and Now*; Stuart Miller and George Nairn, *Around Washington*; Stephen Holley, *Washington Quicker by Quango*; Grigor McLelland, *Washington Over and Out 1983-88*; C.A. Smith, features in the *Sunderland Echo*, February to August 1963.

Finally, I must thank my husband Peter Freeman for help with research and endless support, patience and love. I dedicate this book to him.

Introduction

A stranger arriving on July 4 in Washington Village might well be amazed by the fervour of the Independence Day celebrations which take place every year in its Old Hall. Schoolchildren, villagers and visitors join together in singing the National Anthem of the United States and the Battle Hymn of the Republic, readings include passages from the Declaration of Independence, and the Stars and Stripes flag is raised with due ceremony. And then there is traditional music and dancing in the grounds. So why does this village, tucked away in a rural corner of the New Town that takes its name, within the City of Sunderland in North East England, celebrate the victory of 'the other side' in the American War of Independence? The answer is that the Old Hall is the ancestral home of the family of George Washington, the general leading the victorious American forces and the first President of the United States. This village, as locals will proudly tell you, is 'the original Washington'. It gave the President's family its name – and so, indirectly, gave its name to Washington DC, since the capital of the new country was named after the President in 1791. There is great pride in the bond with America and this was cemented in June, 2006, with the signing of an Agreement of Friendship between Washington DC and Sunderland, in which the two cities will forge new links based on the historic ties.

By 1180, George Washington's direct ancestor, his many-times-great grandfather William, had settled here after agreeing to take over the manor of Washington in an exchange of land with the Bishop of Durham, Hugh Pudsey, who wanted to build a castle and expand his lands in the Stockton area. Following custom, William de Hertburn took the name of his new manor and became William de Washington (or Wessyngton – there were several spellings). Otherwise, the US capital might have been Hertburn DC. Subsequent generations took the surname Washington. Following the English Civil War, one of these, John, emigrated to the New World and settled in Virginia – and his great grandson was George Washington. The family crest of stars and stripes (along with the first American flag) is still displayed in the Old Hall, which has been much rebuilt, but still stands on its original foundations and has retained original stonework, arches and other features. The same crest is carved in the walls of Hylton Castle three miles away, home of the Hylton or Hilton family who intermarried with the Washingtons. The Boldon Book of 1183 (Durham's Domesday Book) records that the Hilton barons held Barmston, with the remaining settlements of the manor of Washington – Usworth, Little Usworth, Biddick and Washington village – held by William de Washington, except for the church and its lands. Generations of Washingtons were baptised in the font of the parish church which today has a corner dedicated to the American connection.

There are many strands to Washington's rich history, with tales of a suspected witch being drowned in the village pond, stories of the notorious highwayman Bob Hazlitt being captured at the village smithy, and of ale being served in the Washington Arms thirty years before Columbus discovered America (more than 500 years later, ale is still consumed here). No story is more amazing than that of Gertrude Bell: born in Dame Margaret Hall in Washington Village in 1868, she gained a First from Lady Margaret Hall, Oxford, became a gifted linguist, explored the deserts of Arabia on horseback, was a First World War heroine, advocated independence for Mesopotamia and is credited with negotiating the foundation of the state of Iraq. Her adventures were financed by money made by her grandfather, Washington industrialist Isaac Lowthian Bell.

The settlements here are best known for their great contribution to industry. Washington was built on a bedrock of coal measures and situated on the River Wear for easy transportation, and great oaks grew in Biddick Wood for the building of the early wooden ships. A dug-out canoe in the collection of Sunderland Museum found on the Washington border dates back 4,000 years, and was chipped out of the solid trunk of an oak tree. In the early nineteenth century, there were five shipbuilding berths at Washington Staithes and two across the river at Coxgreen. The shipyards here closed with the advent of iron ships and the last wooden ship was built here in 1862.

King Coal was the giant industry, and a fine tradition goes back to 1356, when coal was first worked on Washington Moor, though much of the area remained predominantly agricultural until the twentieth century. Washington is notable for a number of industrial 'firsts'. The first steam engine used for draining coal mines was built on the moor by Thomas Newcomen in 1718, though sadly part of a ruined wall is all that is left of the engine house, which was demolished around forty years ago. The first colliery to raise coal to the surface by steam power was at Chatershaugh in 1753, the first pit to have a furnace on the surface to draw foul air up through the shaft was at Biddick in 1756, and the first wagonway to use fixed engines, instead of horses, to haul wagons up an incline was also at Biddick in 1756. In 1812, coal from twenty-three collieries was teemed into keels (flat-bottomed wooden boats) on a two-mile stretch of the River Wear from Lambton to Washington Staithes, and each tide, 300 keels carried their coals down to Sunderland for loading into sea-going colliers.

By the mid-nineteenth century, further prosperity was brought by Washington Chemical Works, whose mountainous white heaps rivalled the black ones of the pits as blots on the landscape. At the Great Exhibition in 1851, Isaac Lowthian Bell showed specimens of magnesia, lead ore, chloride of lead and of silver and a silver plate made at the chemical works, his partner Hugh Lee Pattinson having devised a process for separating silver from lead. At various times, the plant had furnaces for smelting iron and aluminium, and smelting lead for the manufacture of white lead for paint. By the late nineteenth century, this was the largest plant in the world for making magnesia, which was used in talcum powder, cosmetics and in milk of magnesia, the popular indigestion cure. Caustic soda was produced and, long before its dangers were known, asbestos.

In the shadow of these great industries – and the spoil heaps they produced – grew close-knit communities and much of this book is dedicated to photographs of the Washington people of yesteryear at work and play, and of their churches, chapels, shops and traditions, such as the parade of colliery bands and banners to the annual Durham Miners' Gala, which continue to this day.

Just over forty years ago, on 24 July 1964 (in the same week that the Government announced that the first railway to close under the Beeching Plan would be the Washington station to Newcastle line) Washington was designated a New Town. The following year, the board of the new quango, Washington Development Corporation, drew up a master plan. The vision of the future was not universally popular, involving the demolition of a third of the houses, and Fatfield folk in particular campaigned against the proposed decimation of their village. But the end result was a new town made up of individual villages, each with its own architectural character, mixed housing, its own primary and nursery school, village hall, pub, most with shops, and a small amount of industry in each neighbourhood as well as in ten new industrial estates, plus a new town centre incorporating a covered shopping mall with vast free car parks, office blocks, a library, health centre, and sports centre with multi-purpose hall, squash courts, gym and swimming pool. The national census showed this was the biggest growth area in Britain in the decade to 1971 and, by 1988, the original population of 20,000 had grown to 60,000. Thousands more travelled to work or shop. Jobs created reached 22,500 in 1979, then dipped to 18,500 in 1982 – but two years later, Nissan announced Washington was its chosen site in Britain, bringing another 3,400 jobs, plus others in satellite factories, and American companies, including sports giant Nike, brought hundreds more.

A green environment was a priority from the start. Not only did the Development Corporation sweep away the waste heaps and dereliction of the old industries and the sub-standard homes, but they also drew up a master plan for conservation, taking into account the three basic ecological areas – dry heathland to the west, grassland in the centre and deciduous woodland to the south – and listed the appropriate trees and shrubs and their benefit to small wildlife. They even incorporated wildlife corridors in building schemes, with culverts in roads so that small mammals could migrate through to ponds and lakes. They planted 80 million bulbs to herald each spring, and 3.5 million trees, now in their early maturity after forty years. And they created Washington Wildfowl and Wetlands Centre on a 103-acre site which is still evolving as a fine nature reserve and attraction to visitors, on foot or wing. The Development Corporation wound up in 1988 and Washington is now part of the City of Sunderland. It is a success story, despite the early misgivings. But strangers still get lost on the new roads which circle the new town.

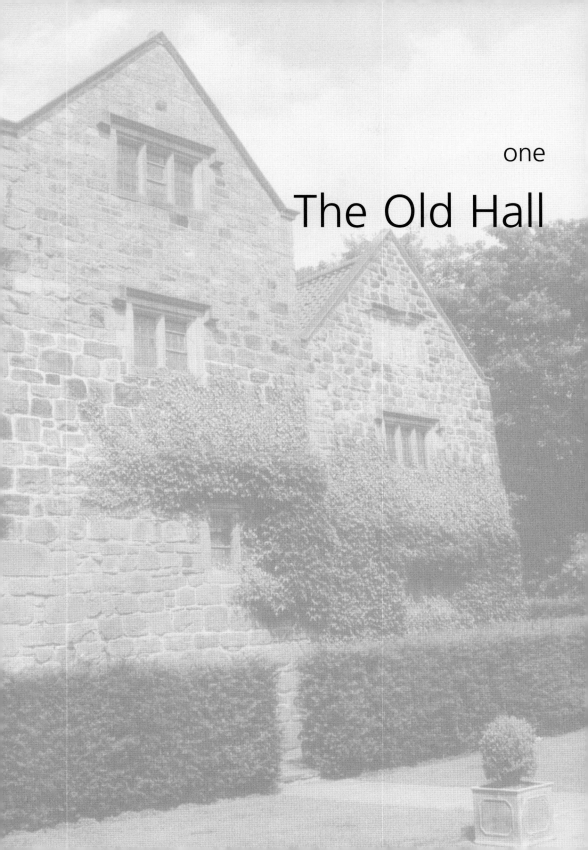

one

The Old Hall

Above and below: The Old Hall in 'the original Washington' – ancestral seat of George Washington, leader of the forces which secured the independence of the American Colonies in the American Revolution, and subsequently first President of the United States in 1789 – is currently the pride of the people of Sunderland. But these pictures show the dereliction into which it had fallen in the 1930s. A preservation committee, with the local schoolmaster and the village rector at its spearhead, was formed to save it.

Above and below: Washington Old Hall has now been beautifully restored, as befits the place which gave its name to the capital city of the United States. To cement the connection, a Friendship Agreement between Washington DC and Sunderland was signed in June 2006 at the British Embassy in the US. The capital was named in honour of George Washington, first President of the United States — and hence after this ancient manor in North East England. George's direct ancestor, William de Hertburn, became William de Washington (or Wessyngton — there were various spellings at the time) on taking over the manor, by 1180, in an exchange of land initiated by the Bishop of Durham, Hugh of Le Puiset (or, more commonly, Pudsey). But for the bishop's whim to build a castle in Hertburn, there might have been a Hertburn DC today. Subsequent generations adopted the surname

Washington, which had several spellings. The Anglo-Saxon word Washington derives from Wassa, a Saxon chief; Inga, the family of; and Tun, the estate. In 1613, another Bishop of Durham, William James, bought the manor of Washington for £4000 and settled it on his youngest son Francis, who rebuilt the hall on the original foundations. The present building is believed to date either from 1613 or 1623, when Francis married, but some of the walls and arches are from the original medieval structure. Overall, the architectural style of the present building belongs to the early seventeenth century when elements of classicism began to permeate the mainstream of English architecture. The hall was opened to the public by the American Ambassador in 1955 and the following year, it was given to the National Trust, which continues to care for it. The hall is open to the public from 1 April to 31 October, from Sunday to Wednesday inclusive, from 11 a.m. to 5 p.m. On the remaining days of the week it is available for weddings and receptions, which help pay for its maintenance.

Above, left and right: The Rector of Washington, the Revd Canon Cyril Lomax (1899-1947) (right) in his riding gear in 1913 and local headmaster Frederick Hill (1885-1955) (left) studying in the shadow of a portrait of George Washington in the 1940s. These formidable gentlemen were the key figures in saving the Old Hall from demolition in 1932, when it was declared unfit for human habitation and a closure order was imposed. The building had been let to a succession of tenants by the late nineteenth century and had slid down the social scale and degenerated to a working class tenement and fallen into dereliction. The preservation committee was formed to raise funds to buy and restore the building. Fred Hill formed a 'Hands Across the Sea' scheme to form friendship links with the United States and in this way involve various American benefactors. Sadly neither Canon Lomax, rector from 1899-1947, nor Mr Hill saw the Old Hall restored. Their preservation committee bought it for £350 in 1937. It finally reopened in September 1955.

Opposite page: Restoration plans were disrupted by the Second World War, but the Old Hall was used as the focal point for events, such as a parade and pageant on 20 May 1941, to raise funds during War Weapons Week. A British soldier escorts the Statue of Liberty, as portrayed by Emily Rodham (later well known as Mrs Forte, having married into the family which had popular ice-cream shops in Washington). George Washington's crest is over the side door of the Old Hall and the United States flag is flying.

Above and below: Restoration began in earnest in 1951, when it was decided that, despite the remaining fragments of the medieval building, the Old Hall should be presented as a seventh-century manor house. Viscount Gort was heavily involved during this phase and the restoration owes much to his generosity and to that of various American benefactors. The hall was opened to the public by the American Ambassador in 1955 and the following year, it was given to the National Trust, which continues to care for it.

COMMITTEE FOR THE
WASHINGTON

PRESERVATION OF
OLD HALL

The Chairman
(The Viscount Gort, M.C., D.L.)
and the
Committee for the Preservation of Washington Old Hall
request the pleasure of your company
at
Washington Old Hall
at 3·0 p.m. on Wednesday, 28th September, 1955
on the occasion of the Opening of the Old Hall
by the
Hon Winthrop W. Aldrich,
U.S. Ambassador to the Court of St. James's

INFORMAL DRESS

The invitation to the reopening of the Old Hall by the Hon. Winthrop W. Aldrich, US Ambassador to the Court of St James, on Wednesday 28 September 1955. The invitation was issued by the chairman, Lord Gort, MC DL, and the Committee for the Preservation of Washington Old Hall. The invitation bore the Washington family crest.

The reopening of the Old Hall attracted enthusiastic crowds as the US Ambassador arrived, escorted by Lord Lawson of Beamish, to inspect the Guard of Honour. This was followed by a prayer of dedication said by the Revd John Lund and then the display of the national flags of Britain and America and the playing of the Star Spangled Banner and God Save the Queen.

Above, left and right: Lord Gort hands the keys to the Old Hall to US Ambassador Winthrop W. Aldrich for the formal opening of the hall to the public on 28 September 1955. On the right, a member of the New York National Guard, sent to escort the US Ambassador, stands to attention for the inspection before the opening ceremony.

Below: The Union Jack and the Stars and Stripes on parade outside the Old Hall with the guard of honour provided by the Washington Greys (the 258th Battalion of the New York National Guard) on 28 September 1955.

THE WASHINGTON GREYS

A poster left by the Washington Greys to mark their visit to the ancient Washington. Their shield is a modification of George Washington's, reversing the colours and using grey piped with gold instead of silver and with red to denote artillery. One company of the New York National Guard paraded as an escort to George Washington on his inauguration as President of the United States on 30 April 1789 and to commemorate this event, assumed the name 'Washington Greys' which it has borne to this day. It was then an artillery organisation and wore a grey uniform – the different styles of uniform over the years are depicted in the poster.

Right: A rather different detachment of Washington Greys bear the Union Jack and the Stars and Stripes on parade behind Washington Welfare Hall in the 1960s. The name was adopted in honour of the American connection by this local juvenile jazz band, of a type popular in the middle of the twentieth century. Instruments included bazookas and kazoos.

17

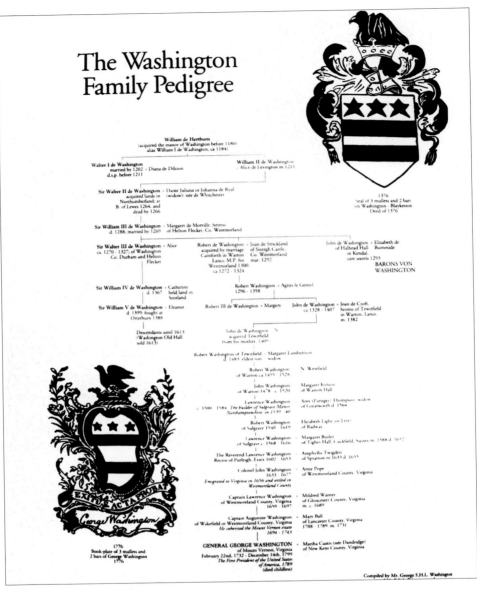

The Washington Family Pedigree

William de Hertburn
(acquired the manor of Washington before 1180)
alias William I de Washington, ca 1184)

Walter I de Washington
married by 1202 · Diana de Dilston
d.s.p. before 1211

William II de Washington · Alice de Lexington m.1211

1376
Seal of 3 mullets and 2 bars
on Washington · Blaykeston
Deed of 1376

Sir Walter II de Washington · Dame Juliana or Johanna de Ryal
acquired lands in (widow) née de Whitchester
Northumberland; at
B. of Lewes 1264, and
dead by 1266

Sir William III de Washington · Margaret de Morville, heiress
d. 1288; married by 1269 of Helton Flecket, Co. Westmorland

Sir Walter III de Washington · Alice
ca 1270 - 1327, of Washington
Co. Durham and Helton
Flecket

Robert de Washington · Joan de Strickland
acquired by marriage of Sizergh Castle,
Carnforth in Warton Co. Westmorland
Lancs. M.P. for mar. 1292
Westmorland 1300;
ca 1272 - 1324

John de Washington · Elizabeth de
of Halhead Hall Burneside
in Kendal
jure uxoris 1293

**BARONS VON
WASHINGTON**

Sir William IV de Washington · Catherine
d. 1367 held land in
Scotland

Robert Washington · Agnes le Gentyl
1296 - 1358

Sir William V de Washington · Eleanor
d. 1399; fought at
Otterburn 1388

Robert III de Washington · Margery

John de Washington · Joan de Croft,
ca 1328 - 1407 heiress of Tewitfield
in Warton, Lancs.
m. 1382

Descendants until 1613
(Washington Old Hall
sold 1613)

John de Washington
acquired Tewitfield
from his mother, 1409

Robert Washington of Tewitfield · Margaret Lambertson
d. 1483 eldest son widow

Robert Washington · N. Westfield
of Warton ca 1455 - 1528

John Washington · Margaret Kytson
of Warton 1478 - c. 1520 of Warton Hall

Lawrence Washington · Amy (Pargiter) Thompson, widow
c. 1500 - 1584 *The builder of Sulgrave Manor* of Greatworth d. 1564
Northamptonshire in 1539 - 40

Robert Washington · Elizabeth Light (or Lyte)
of Sulgrave 1540 - 1619 of Radway

Lawrence Washington · Margaret Butler
of Sulgrave c. 1568 - 1616 of Tighes Hall, Cuckfield, Sussex m. 1588 d. 1652

The Reverend Lawrence Washington · Amphyllis Twigden
Rector of Purleigh, Essex 1602 - 1653 of Spratton m. 1633 d. 1655

Colonel John Washington · Anne Pope
1633 - 1677 of Westmoreland County, Virginia
*Emigrated to Virginia in 1656 and settled in
Westmoreland County*

Captain Lawrence Washington · Mildred Warner
of Westmoreland County, Virginia of Gloucester County, Virginia
1659 - 1697 m. c. 1689

Captain Augustine Washington · Mary Ball
of Wakefield in Westmoreland County, Virginia of Lancaster County, Virginia
He inherited the Mount Vernon estate 1708 - 1789, m. 1731
1694 - 1743

GENERAL GEORGE WASHINGTON · Martha Custis (née Dandridge)
of Mount Vernon, Virginia of New Kent County, Virginia
February 22nd, 1732 - December 14th, 1799
*The First President of the United States
of America, 1789*
(died childless)

1776
Book-plate of 3 mullets and
2 bars of George Washington
1776

George Washington

EXITUS ACTA PROBAT

Compiled by Mr. George S.H.L. Washington

Above and opposite above: The crest of George Washington on a bookplate dated 1776, below left on this Washington family pedigree, is clearly derived from the Washington family seal of 1376, above right. The Washington family pedigree traces the lineage of George Washington back to that of William de Hertburn, who, in the days before surnames, became William de Washington on taking over the ancient manor, by 1180, in an exchange with the Bishop of Durham, Hugh of Le Puiset (1153-95). Because of its American connection, Washington Old Hall has a comprehensive collection of portraits of George Washington and illustrations of events connected with the struggle for American Independence. Many items have been given by American benefactors. The Stars and Stripes (at the top of the opposite page) bears the thirteen stars of the thirteen original states in the Union, and regularly flies from the flagpost at Washington Old Hall.

Above, left and right: A view of the Old Hall from the gardens and a section of the Jacobean garden which echoes the symmetry of the building. The original medieval structure was rebuilt of local, honey-coloured sandstone in a typical early seventeenth-century 'H' plan. The original entrance faced the church and it is there that the symmetry of the building is most apparent. In the most recent stage of the restoration, the Jacobean gardens have been recreated. In the lower walled garden the compartments or parterres are filled with old English flowers and herbs in common use during the seventeenth century, not only for decorative but also for medicinal and culinary purposes. The Mead is an area of semi-wildness used in the seventeenth century as a place for quiet contemplation. Here a plena tree (*prunus avium*) has been planted in memory of those who perished in the Twin Towers of New York on 11 September 2001 – another echo of the closeness felt with the Old Hall's American connection.

This panelled room in the Old Hall would have been a private family room at the dais end of the Great Hall. The fine Jacobean panelling came from an old manor house and is made of quartered oak. The English long-case clock dating from around 1688 has marquetry inlay in a pattern, widely used as a decorative feature in the Stuart period. The stump workbox dates from the middle of the seventeenth century and depicts the flight of Mary and Joseph.

In its rebuilt state, the Old Hall had five bedrooms and a linen closet upstairs and to the western end stood a milk house and buttery. Subsequent remodelling has obscured the original arrangement. The oak bed in this bedroom is either Flemish or German and has cupboards in both ends for the concealment of weapons and valuables. The flanking candlestands are Dutch and date from the seventeenth century. The baby walker demonstrates that more than three centuries ago, people were using the same method as used today to help teach babies to walk.

It is believed that most or even all of the walls of the kitchen in the Old Hall date from the medieval building. Visitors see it today as it would have looked during the Stuart period. Note the large spit for cooking over the open fire. On the table is a selection of dishes taken from *The Accomplisht Cook* published in 1664. These include apple tansey, pigeon fricasse and almond pudding. Ingredients on display include cinnamon, ginger and nutmeg, all

extensively used in the sweet and savoury dishes of the period. The design of the pottery is taken from contemporary London ware, which would have been brought into the Washington area as part of the return loads of the collier brigs, which required plenty of ballast on the stormy North Sea.

The Great Hall would have been the centre of the household's life as well as the communal eating place. A platform would have been sited at the eastern end, away from the bustle and smell of the kitchen and close to the warmth of the fire. The family and important guests would have taken their meal here, with retainers eating at a central table. The fireplace was given

during the restoration of the hall by Lord Gort and came from Newburn Manor on the River Tyne. The heavy robust furniture is typically Jacobean, predominantly made of oak and carved in high relief. The chairs date from 1660 and the central table is from the early part of the seventeenth century and has a loose top. The stools around it would have been stored under the table when not in use. Various pieces of Delftware are on display which would have been imported from Holland, with whom there were strong trading links during this period.

Above and below: Independence Day is celebrated with gusto at Washington Old Hall, often with quintessentially English elements as with the Morris dancers, above. Children always play a big role, and here there is a display of English country dancing, shortly after the maypole dancing class at Columbia Primary School finished their entertainment in 1993, when the youngsters were also celebrating 100 years of their school building (originally called Biddick). Celebrations in 2006, organised by the National Trust and Washington School, included an address by the Mayor, Cllr Tom Foster, to mark the newly-signed Friendship Agreement with Washington DC. The United States flag was raised by Patricia Everts of the Daughters of the American Revolution, there was a reading from the Declaration of Independence and rousing renditions of The Star Spangled Banner and The Battle Hymn of the Republic.

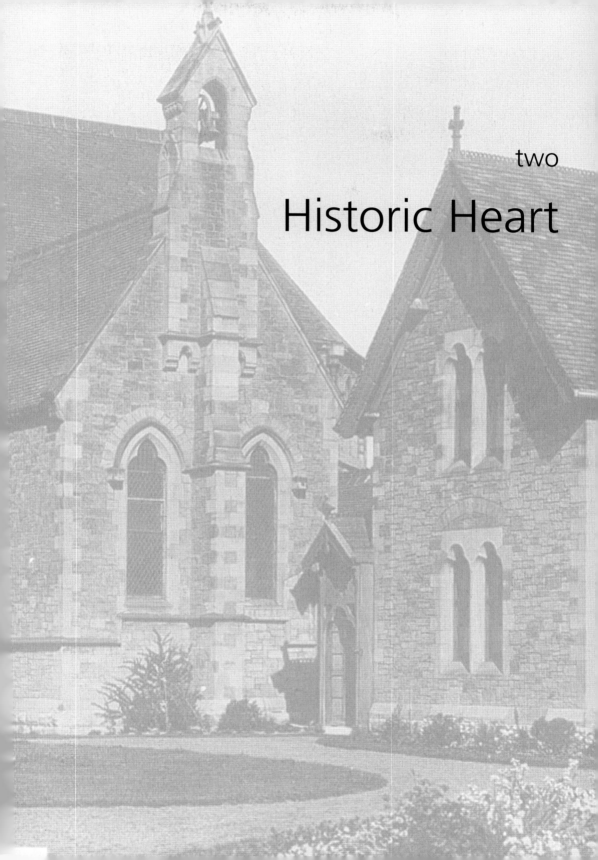

two

Historic Heart

Washington Village Green, the historic heart of the community, before the First World War. On the left is a horse and cart delivering beer to the Cross Keys Inn. The old police station (now a guest house called Ye Olde Cop Shoppe) which accommodated the police sergeant and six constables, is in the centre, and to the left is a shop (now Washington Green public library) advertising on its gable end, Fry's and Cadbury's cocoa.

A pre-First World War view of Washington parish church showing two women and children at the entrance from The Avenue, with the old smithy to the left. The old stocks, for confining drunkards and delinquents, once stood between the smithy and the church. There has been a church on this tree-clad slope for a thousand years and possibly a pagan site on the mound before that (though only excavation could prove its early history). When George Washington's many-times-great-grandfather William arrived some time before 1180, he took over the whole of the manor, with the exception of the church and its lands, and Barmston, held by the Hilton barons. The church at that time was surrounded by a moat, formed partly by Washington Beck, which rose as a spring (the Spout from which Spout Lane takes its name), flowed south to a pond, and continued west of the church before turning sharply eastwards.

Holy Trinity church in the 1950s with its bell tower dating back to the 1830s still intact. There is little trace left of the Norman church and its medieval additions and subsequent alterations at the time of the Reformation. The old church was pulled down in 1832 after a survey by architect John Green found it insecure. Research by the historian Margot Johnson shows the pillars and arches dividing the nave from the aisles were out of perpendicular and at 21ft were overhanging by some twelve inches. The west wall, 24ft high, overhung seventeen inches from top to bottom. John Green was commissioned to design a new church, re-using material wherever possible. But there were complaints from the start, not least that the new pews were uncomfortable and a radical enlargement took place in which the belfry was moved to the west. The church was reopened in 1883.

The church and village centre shown in November 1962, in the early snow of a bitter winter and in the month that the new £7,000 bell turret, added to the west end of the nave, was dedicated by Bishop Stephen Bayne. The new copper spire was placed in position by a helicopter, to some excitement. At that time the porch was remodelled, the medieval doorway moved to the centre of the west wall and the gallery stairs reversed. The church is now known as Holy Trinity, though earlier it was known as St Mary's. The earliest documents, however, give no indication of a name.

The Washington corner in the parish church, with the twelfth-century font in which generations of the Washingtons were baptised. This font had been discarded in one of the radical alterations of the church and had been replaced by a new font in Frosterley marble. The ancient font was rescued from Manor House Farm where it was being used as a drinking trough for animals. It was reinstated in the 'American corner' which also bears a portrait of George Washington, sent from the United States through headmaster Frederick Hill's Hands Across the Sea scheme. The baptistery window's stained glass, showing children being brought to Jesus for blessing here, was given in memory of Fred Hill, 1885-1955, historian of Washington and promoter of the Old Hall and of Anglo-American friendship. Descendants of George Washington commissioned a stained-glass window for the nave, bearing the family crest and completed by the great glass artist Leonard Evetts in 1961.

Even the Mothers' Union banner adopted the stars and stripes of the Washington family crest. This 1940s picture shows Mrs Minto, centre, the enrolling member for the parish church Mothers' Union with the two oldest members, Mrs Ross and Mrs Humble.

The rector, Canon Cyril Lomax, ready to set out on horseback on his rounds in the predominantly rural parish in the 1930s. His dog was ready to go, too. Canon Lomax was Rector of Washington from 1899 to 1946 and he never had a car. Children vied with one another to hold the horse's reins when the rector dismounted and he would reward them with coins.

Above: Village Lane looking towards the crossroads in 1903, as a horse-drawn cart makes its way down the street watched by children and villagers. The old Chantry House is to the right of the church.

Above: Dame Margaret Hall, built to the south of Washington Old Hall by the industrialist Sir Isaac Lowthian Bell and completed in 1857, with a host of idiosyncratic architectural features. This was the birthplace of his granddaughter, local heroine Gertrude Bell, who explored the deserts of Arabia on horseback. A gifted linguist, she served as an intelligence officer in the First World War and afterwards represented Britain in negotiations with the Arabs. She advocated independence for Mesopotamia and so was a key figure in the founding of the independent state of Iraq. She died in Baghdad in 1926, aged fifty-eight.

Right: Close-up of a carved dog, one of the many decorative features on the walls of Dame Margaret Hall.

Opposite below: Architectural details in Dame Margaret Hall, with the carved crest above the doorway, left, and on the right, the oriel window with the inscription: 'This house was created by I. Lowthian Bell in the years 1854 and 1857'. Isaac Lowthian Bell was an eminent local industrialist and he built his hall, originally called Washington House, to the south of the Old Hall. Its brickwork was decorated with gargoyles, crockets, arches and tracery, believed to have been from the old church which was pulled down in 1832.

CATHOLIC CHURCH AND MANSE, WASHINGTON. (851)

The Roman Catholic church of Our Lady, with the west end of the Presbytery. Washington was always well served with churches.

Looking east along Village Lane with St Joseph's School on the right, in a view taken before the First World War.

A large crowd gathered for the ceremony when Lord Durham unveiled the war memorial on the village green in 1920. The names of villagers who died in the Second World War have joined those who were killed in the First World War.

Children pose round the war memorial in the 1930s while old men gather in the shelter to the left. The parish church and blacksmith's shop are in the background.

The eighteenth-century rectory in 1937 when it was taken over to serve as the second council offices. Before the founding of the New Town, Washington was served by an Urban District Council as part of the administrative County of Durham. The rectory was destroyed by fire in 1949.

New council offices were built to replace the old rectory after the disastrous fire. The architectural style was meant to echo that of the rectory.

The Washington Arms, more than 500 years old, is the oldest pub in the area. It is said that ale was served here thirty years before Columbus discovered America.

An Edwardian view of the Cross Keys Inn, a neighbouring rival of the Washington Arms facing the village green.

Above: Staff and customers outside the Black Bush Inn on the south side of Village Lane, probably in the 1940s.

Below: This is a view looking south-east towards the war memorial, with the parish church of Holy Trinity in the background. Once, there was a village pond here where, in 1676, legend has it that a suspected witch called Jane Atkinson was drowned after summary trial on the green. But Jane was a prominent pew holder in the parish church and the burial entry states *Praestigiatrix (ut aiunt)* – a practitioner, so they say. The historian Margot Johnson says ordinary medical practice was so described and the legend that Jane was a witch is unfounded.

Above and below: The oldest known picture of the blacksmith's, taken in the late nineteenth century. Strategically placed in the centre of Washington village, it was convenient for travellers staying at local inns, as well as local farmers and landowners. For many years the blacksmiths here were members of the Dobson family and that is believed to be Mr Dobson pictured below on the right. It was here that the notorious highwayman Bob Hazlitt was captured in 1770 after his smart grey mare was recognised by a post boy who had seen it in action at a mail coach robbery on Wrekenton Long Bank. Hazlitt was tried at Durham, hanged, and his body brought back to be displayed on a gibbet at Wrekenton as a warning to others.

Customers line up outside the smithy in the early 1920s, one cart belonging to Royal Standard Oil and the other to A. Thompson, a contractor from Sunderland. The lamp-post bears a sign saying 'Horse buses stop here for Sunderland'. In 1955, the centuries-old smithy was earmarked for conversion to a filling station. It was rescued by Mrs Victor Morawetz, of New York, who sent £350 to Cllr Theodore Nicholson and Lord Gort (then secretary and chairman of the Committee for the Preservation of the Old Hall) asking them to buy it and put it to good use. They took out covenants with the Council for the Preservation of Rural England, to ensure that the smithy building and site would be preserved in perpetuity. The building became a pottery, then a café, and is now the Blacksmith's Table restaurant.

An idyllic view of the peaceful village centre of Washington in 1950, looking across to the police station and the historic Washington Arms. The war memorial is on the left and the blacksmith's shop on the right.

three

Around the Villages

Above and below: These houses along the waggonway at Fatfield were built at least by the early nineteenth century and the daily lives of the early residents would be punctuated by the rolling of the tubs full of coal from the colliery to the staithes on the River Wear. Here they would be loaded into keelboats bound for sea-going colliers waiting in the harbour at Sunderland. The houses stood well below the level of the waggonway; the housewife above, standing outside her home in Ferryboat Cottages, is cut off by the tops of her legs and Waggonway Terrace, below, seems even lower. These pictures were taken in 1934, when the waggons had stopped rolling, thanks to the later rail network. The houses were demolished in the 1930s but a later terrace was also named after the waggonway! An old folk song goes "Clap hands for Daddy, coming down the waggonway/ His pockets full of money and his hands all clay". Pockets were not really so full of money, however.

More substantial houses in Fatfield are shown here in Jerry Yard in 1906 or 1907. The Edwardian lady on the right is Jane Spoors, née Davidson, the grandmother of keen local history buff David Young, to whom the picture belongs.

Above and below: Two views of Slate Houses – yet another prosaic street name – in the 1930s, when families lived with manacles and chains on the walls, left behind by the nineteenth-century lock-up which occupied the premises before them. Above, a billboard on the back yard wall advertises the 1934 New Washington Carnival, open daily, with attractions including 'John Powell, England's super funfair, the new supreme motorcycle speedway and the jubilee waltzer with lightning swirl'. The housewife in the doorway on the left is watching as her children play in the small front garden. Adorning the wall of the house below is a tin bath, used by miners to bathe in front of the fire after a hard shift in the days before pit baths, and by the families living here in the 1930s.

Above: John Thomas Flannigan, with his son on horseback, outside his temperance bar and tea rooms, which he converted from the pub (possibly called the Bird in the Bush) formerly occupying the premises, and of which he may have been landlord before 'seeing the light' in the late nineteenth century. His temperance bar stood beside the riverbanks to the east of Fatfield Bridge.

Below: Customers dressed ready for an outing, complete with waistcoats, cloth caps and even a few trilby hats, are pictured outside the Stile Inn in New Washington in the early twentieth century. Thomas Noble was the landlord, licensed to sell beer, wines, spirits and tobacco... possibly a greater attraction than the temperance bar above.

This is the new Stile Inn on the corner of Station Road, after the village of New Washington was renamed Concord by the Washington Development Corporation. More than forty years on, only 'incomers' call it Concord, natives preferring the old name.

The new Ferryboat Inn at Fatfield in the early twentieth century, with customers and children and the landlord, John Todd, in shirt sleeves and waistcoat, in the centre of the picture. Compare this with the old inn on the opposite page.

A rather younger John Todd, the landlord, in shirt sleeves, stands outside the older version of his Ferryboat Inn, with customers on bicycles. The new inn, opposite, was built on the same site.

There were coke ovens at the end of the street when this Victorian terrace was built – so it seemed natural to call it Coke Ovens. No 'Mon Repos' or 'Shangri-la' in those days, and no bathrooms or indoor toilets either.

This was Low Chapel Row, Fatfield, in 1934, with an old mangle standing in one back yard and washing hanging out next door. There are rugs hanging over the walls for their ritual airing and beating and an old man arriving home at the end of the street. But life round here was once literally vitriolic, for the street stood near Copperas House where green vitriol – the old name for sulphuric acid – was used in tanning and making ink and papier maché for the Ford Paper Mills down the river. David Young reports that it was 'a stinking process, because the materials were laid outdoors for six months to putrefy before being used'.

Local builder Henry Spoors is pictured back left with workmen outside No. 1 Biddick Lane, the street he was building at the time. The local coal merchant Alfie Smith is pictured front left. The picture was taken in 1931.

Children play outside the Edith Avenue flats built by Washington Urban District Council shortly before the establishment of Washington Development Corporation. No prizes for guessing that the new homes built by Henry Spoors thirty years earlier were much more popular.

Above left: Quarrying was one of the main industries in Springwell, so it is not surprising that many of the houses, like this one, were built of stone.

Above right: Staff in the butchering department of the Co-operative store in Washington Station pose for this picture taken in 1912. Washington Development Corporation renamed the village Columbia.

Cecil Butt outside his ironmonger's shop in Victoria Road, a business he established in 1912. It was an Aladdin's cave of household goods. Note the tin bath on the pavement and the line of aluminium cans hanging outside.

The substantial Springwell Co-operative Stores, with staff outside, at around the time of the First World War. Co-op stores were by then established in almost every colliery village and sold everything from food to drapery.

In the early twentieth century, a camera was unusual enough to make children stand still and to bring men out of the reading rooms in Bowes Crescent, Springwell.

Prospect Terrace in Front Street, Springwell, with a horse-drawn dray making a beer delivery to the Perseverance Arms next door to the local Co-operative store. Note the unmade road on this 'Auty series' postcard from around the turn of the twentieth century.

A view of Prospect Terrace taken around thirty years later than the photograph above. The Co-op has been extended and the Perseverance Arms revamped. The changing of the rear wheel of a car attracts the interest of onlookers, including a policeman.

Mr Rutherford stands in the doorway of his grocery and provisions store in Spout Lane. The bargain of the day appears to be Rowntree's cocoa at fourpence halfpenny.

A fine display of cloth caps on the left and of blouses and finery on the right in the windows of Birtley and District Co-op's drapery department in 1911. Two members of staff stand outside and a couple of likely lads are keen to be in the picture too.

Above and below: The Johnson brothers, Arthur and Tom, ran several general dealer's stores. This one is in Spout Lane but there were at least two others, in Council Terrace, New Washington and Emerson Terrace, Glebe. The fine display of Heinz salad cream, below, is in the window of the New Washington (Concord) branch.

Above and below: Ice-cream parlours were popular in the colliery villages, and none more so than those run by the Forte family, who founded their business here in 1920. Standing in the doorway of the shop in Station Terrace, Usworth, in 1922 is Mr Giovanni Forte, his sister Maria and daughter Mary. They also ran the billiard saloon next door. In the earlier picture above can be seen customers Matty Bolam, Tom Nayden and Henry Bannister. Below, fifty years on, standing in the doorway of the ice-cream and confectioner's in Victoria Road, is Mr Guilio Forte, son of the founder.

Above left: Walter Willson's Everywhere says the sign on the gable end of this Washington store and the legend was literally true in the North East, where Walter Willson's stores were ubiquitous until the march of the supermarkets began in the 1960s.

Above right: The landlord, Robert Clark, and his wife pictured around 1900 in the doorway of the new Victoria Hotel, the old one having been situated at Cook's ironworks in Victoria Place.

Swans from nearby Barmston Willows pond were regular visitors to this Walter Willson's, next to the Celtic Club in Station Road.

Staff at W. Pattison, the grocer's, known as 'the Busy Little Shop' in Washington Station, on 4 July 1917. Mrs Pattison is on the left and the errand boy is called Charlton. The shop was next to Glebe School, later renamed John F. Kennedy Primary – yet another American connection.

Fine cuts of meat, black puddings and sausages on display in the window of A. Bell, the family butcher, opposite Freddie Bell's shop in Spout Lane, just north of the crossroads in Washington Village. These shopkeepers were ancestors of the Bell family of Columbia, who later ran a catering business.

Looking west along the unmade road along Front Street in Usworth Village, with Jackson's Buildings centre right and the Red Lion Inn beyond. With modernisations over the years, Front Street remained the heart of the old village until the Development Corporation came along.

This was Albany Village Centre in May 1975. Washington Development Corporation, a quango created by the Wilson Government in 1964, created the New Town with The Galleries shopping complex, library, sports centre, health centre and offices in the town centre and a series of eighteen villages, like Albany, each with its own distinctive architectural style and each with a network of footpaths leading to the village centre, with a local pub and village hall, most with shops, and with limited industry in the neighbourhood. The aim was to foster the community spirit which had sustained the old colliery villages through hard times.

This was the main shopping street in New Washington in the 1950s, with shops including Davidson's the butcher, Duncan's grocers, the post office and even Jones, the department store. Shopping was a social occasion in the old close-knit villages.

This was the new heart of New Washington, renamed Concord by the Development Corporation. The bus station is round the corner on the left. Shops here included Moore's stores, a large Boots, and even a Woolworth's. None of the original shops survive thirty years on, many having been replaced by charity shops. Even the Development Corporation was taken by surprise by the popularity of The Galleries, especially after the arrival of Woolco in 1973. It had 1,000 free car parking spaces outside and at 104,800 square feet of shop floor; it was the biggest store on one level in the country at the time, and drew shoppers from a wide area outside the New Town.

Above and below: Not surprisingly, the pubs, albeit much revamped to cater for today's tastes and now serving food as well as drinks, are the greatest survivors of the old days. These two pubs are on the pleasant riverside at Biddick. The Havelock, above, was named after the nineteenth-century Sunderland-born General dubbed 'hero of Lucknow' for his role in suppressing the Indian mutiny. The Inn Between, below, was formerly the Co-op building of 1909, between the Biddick Inn and the Havelock Arms. The building was converted to a pub in the early 1980s. It had a change of name to the Riverside, then back again to the Inn Between. It is now the River Bar.

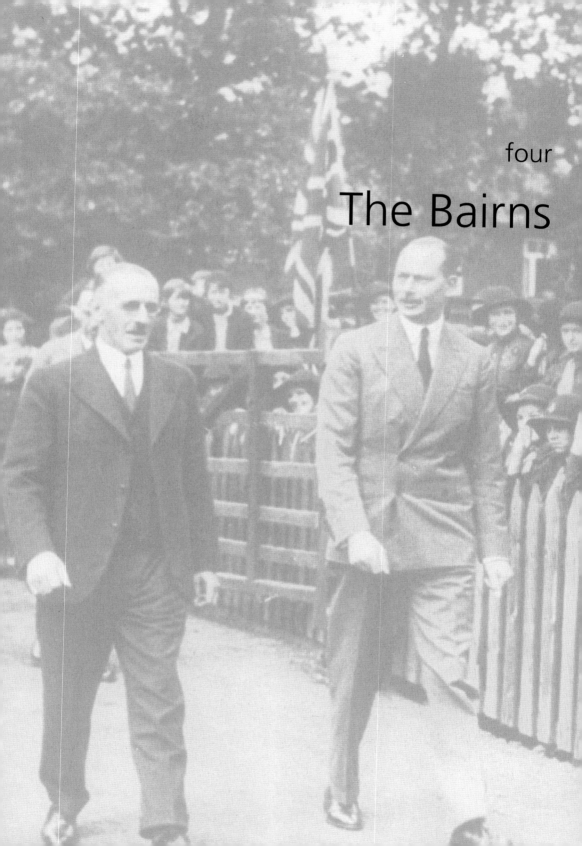

four

The Bairns

Biddick School at the turn of the twentieth century. Mr Turnbull, the master, was killed in an accident at Washington Station.

Everyone sitting to attention at their desks, ink wells full, pens at the ready, in this class at Glebe School around 1910.

The prize-winning football team from Washington Secondary School in 1912. The proud masters are dressed formally for the team photograph.

Here is a class at Bobby Lee's School, Washington Village. No doubt the children were well versed in the story of George Washington's family links with their village.

Above and below: Chapel and church events played a big part in children's lives during much of the 20th century. These are youngsters outside Washington Station Chapel in around 1920 and Joan Nichols, who provided the photographs, believes the picture above is related to the annual May Queens event, while below, the children are probably from the Sunday School. Chapel anniversary entertainments, with children taking turns to sing or recite poetry, and Sunday School treats were highlights of the year.

Right: This is the netball team in the school yard at Glebe School in 1920. No team strips in those days and indeed there is quite an assortment of dress here.

Below: This is Fatfield School in 1919 in a treasured photograph kept by Nora Spoors, who is on the right in the back row. The children look very solemn in these early pictures – perhaps nobody had told them that these were the happiest days of their lives.

Above: The centre of villages, almost traffic-free, were great playgrounds for local children. Here schoolboys play rugby around Washington village green between the wars.

Below: Another picture of Fatfield School, this time in 1922. Right in the middle of the back row is Bobby Thompson, who became a popular local comedian known as 'the Little Waster'. He topped the bill at theatres in the 1950s and latterly was much in demand on the working men's club circuit.

Above and below: The school dog, in the same position on the left of the front row in both pictures, seemed to enjoy having his photograph taken. Above, the priest and one of the teachers, with a class of children, and below, the same priest with a group of teachers in Edwardian finery, at St Bede's RC School, Usworth. Bede, greatest scholar of his day, is a local saint, born at Monkwearmouth and a monk in the split-site Anglo Saxon monastery of St Peter, Monkwearmouth and St Paul, Jarrow.

Above left: The back lane in Castle Street, Fatfield, is a favourite playground for John Wanless, centre, and his brother (left) and friend, here dressed for a game of cowboys and Indians.

Above right: This is John Wanless and his brother again, this time playing city slickers, with the Chatershaugh pit shaft in the background. Industry was always the backdrop to playtimes in the old colliery villages.

Children enjoy a ride on the old roundabout in Usworth Colliery Park playground, in front of the local junior and infant school. The miners' welfare hall is on the left. Miners' welfare organisations provided sports and leisure facilities, often including reading rooms, for their communities.

Street games are being enjoyed by Washington Village children in 1908 in this picture taken from the crossroads of Spout Lane and Village Lane. Note the white pinafores worn by most of the girls.

Sunday School children at the Cook Memorial Church in Brady Square. One of the teachers in this picture, taken after the Second World War, is Joan Nichols.

Above and below: Prince Henry, Duke of Gloucester, arrives for the opening of the youth activities hut in Glebe Crescent in the 1930s, above, watched by a guard of Girl Guides, while below, the Scout troop poses with Mr Cole, representing Newalls chemical works, outside the Geoffrey Newall Hut.

Above and below: Youngsters wearing their sports uniform of vests and baggy shorts go through their paces on the horse, above, and pose for a picture in the gymnasium at Glebe School during the Second World War, below.

Cheery pupils pose outside Washington Grammar School in the 1950s, in their distinctive bottle green uniforms. One of their number is Joan Nichols.

Casually dressed youngsters leave the new Albany Junior School in the 1970s, before the swing back to school uniforms.

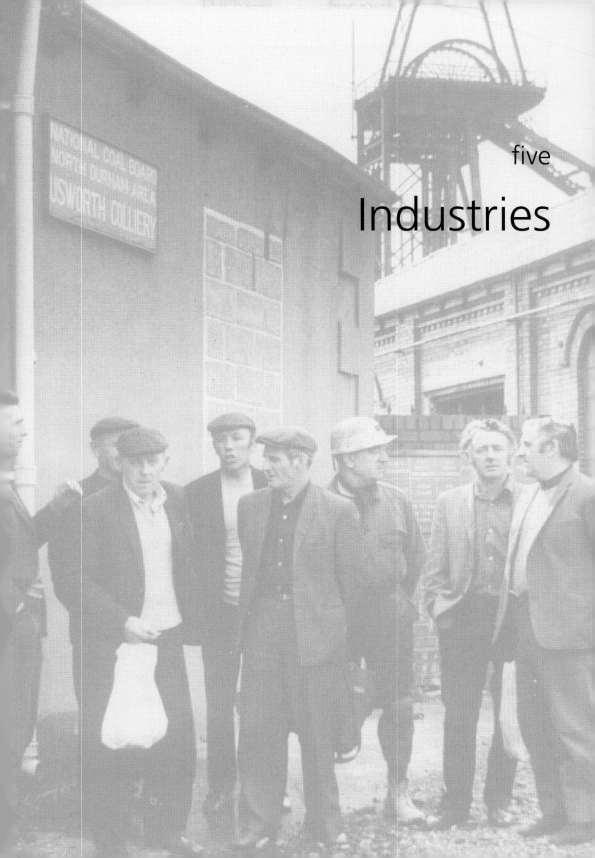

five

Industries

Above and below: For many centuries, farming was the predominant industry around Washington. Usworth House Farm, above and below, survived until the advent of the Washington Development Corporation, which demolished even the ancient tithe barn adjoining the farm buildings. The bar was where the tithe, or one-tenth, of produce owing to the lord of the manor was stored in feudal times. Dobbin the horse, just visible in the picture below, was famous for escaping a Second World War bomb which killed his companions.

Above: Much of Washington remained rural until late in the twentieth century and indeed parts remain so today. This is a tractor-hauled reaper working on Baxter's Farm, Washington, around 1960. Compare this pleasant aspect with the scene below.

Below: The chemical works dominated the houses in Washington Staithes. This was one of the first parts of the area to be despoiled, being the terminus for waggonways bringing coal from the pits, and also the site of five shipbuilding berths. The last ship was built in Washington in 1862. The larger iron ships being introduced required a greater draught than was available on the inland stretch of the River Wear. Coxgreen is in the foreground below.

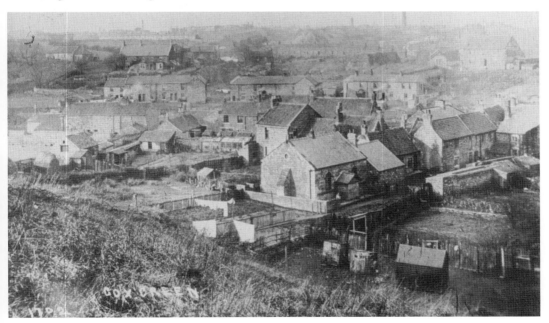

The chemical works established in Washington in 1840 brought greater prosperity to the area, but much of the work was hard, stifling and unpleasant. These women, pictured around 1880, are cutting moulded magnesia into blocks in the magnesia loft at the works while sunlight streams in through the cell-like

windows. By the late nineteenth century, this was the largest plant in the world for making magnesia, which was used in talcum powder, cosmetics and milk of magnesia, the indigestion remedy.

Above: The kilns of Washington Chemical Works, used for burning limestone during the Leblanc caustic soda process, and the tank waste dump. At various times, the plant had furnaces for smelting iron and aluminium, and smelting lead for the manufacture of white pigment for paint. Its heaviest raw materials were close at hand; coal came from local pits and the plant was built near magnesian limestone. The whole of the area was landscaped by Washington Development Corporation and not a trace remains.

Below: The wasteland around the chemical works, *c.* 1870. The chimney left of the furnace was built in 1850. The picture shows the top of the waste heaps. The alkali waste was produced during the Leblanc caustic soda process where common salt is decomposed using sulphuric acid. The resultant sulphate is heated with chalk and small coal in a furnace then lixiviated with water, evaporated and calcined with sawdust. The soda ash produced is dissolved and crystallised to give caustic soda. Huge quantities of waste were produced. The white mountains of the chemical works rivalled the black ones of the pits as blots on the landscape – but not a trace of them is now left.

This is the earliest known photograph of Washington Chemical Works, established in 1840 by Hugh Lee Pattinson (after whom a local township is named) in partnership with metallurgist and industrialist Isaac Lowthian Bell. At the Great Exhibition in 1851, Bell showed specimens of magnesia, lead ore, chloride of lead and of silver, and a silver plate made at the chemical works, his partner Pattinson having devised a process for separating silver from lead. Pattinson's daughter married another local industrialist, Robert Stirling Newall, famous for wire rope-making and devising machinery for laying submarine cable, including 1,250 miles of the first cable between Britain and America. By 1872, Newall was sole owner of the chemical works which was known as Newall's until it closed in the 1980s, although it had become Turner and Newall.

The chemical works was making asbestos by 1929 and this is possibly the load on this Albion lorry about to leave the garage. Asbestos was regarded as a wonder material long before its hazards were known.

Above: This picture taken from Holy Trinity churchyard at High Usworth shows work begun on Donwell Village in 1967. It is also an example of how pits and pit heaps, in this case Washington F pit, came to dominate landscape. Now not a single pit heap remains here.

Below: This is the headgear, buildings, waggons and tubs of Washington F pit. It was the sixth pit sunk on the site by 1777, all named after letters of the alphabet. At a depth of 678ft it was one of the earliest working deep mines in the country. After nationalisation, the shaft was sunk to 929ft to reach the Busty seam. The pit reached its peak in the mid-1960s, with 1,500 men producing 486,000 tons of coal in 1964–65 but not enough to save it from closure three years later. The last coal was drawn on 21 June 1968.

Above and below: To work and back in the open coble boat which served as the ferry near the Victoria rail bridge. The ferry took miners living on the south bank at Penshaw to work at North Biddick Colliery across the River Wear. The picture above was taken in 1920 and miners in the boat include Bob Richardson, third left, and Joe Brewer, and the picture below was taken a few years later. The ferryman is the same. This area of the river was nicknamed Botany (pronounced 'Butney' locally) Bay and hence the mine was known as Butney pit.

This Usworth Lodge banner of 1955 shows Keir Hardie, first Independent Labour MP in 1892 and champion of trade union rights. Its motto read: Emancipation of Labour. It was the Lodge's third banner, first unfurled on the eve of the 1955 Durham Miners' Gala by Mr Maguire, who had been Lodge delegate. Every miners' lodge had its own distinctive banner, many of them celebrating early heroes of the labour movement and they would all be paraded at the annual Durham Miners' Gala on the second Saturday of every July. Even today communities raise money to replace old and worn banners and have new ones made, elaborately worked in silk. They bear legends exhorting their followers to fight for a better life, such as 'The Past We Inherit, The Future We Build; Education Is Our Future; Take Up The Task Eternal, The Burden and The Lesson'.

Above and below: Sunday best was the dress code for the annual outing to the Durham Miners' Gala in July, as these mining families from Washington F pit demonstrate as they pose on the riverside at Durham at the 1930 Gala. They would listen to the speeches and then have a picnic and a get-together with friends from far-flung pits they hadn't seen since the previous year. In the days before cars, this was the one day of the year when families were reunited. As the picture below shows, formal dress remained the norm even after the Second World War. This was the Glebe banner about to be paraded in Emerson Terrace; most lodges followed their band and banner round their locality before going to the Gala. Identified in this picture are Jim Hall, the tallest man centre left of the banner, Jack Kelley in the flat cap on the right of the banner and Johnson Palmer in the flat cap nearest the camera to the right of the banner.

Washington Staithes pictured at the turn of the twentieth century with a lunar landscape of waste heaps from the chemical works behind homes where washing billows on the lines. By the beginning of the nineteenth century, twenty-three collieries were teeming their coals into keels on a two-mile stretch of the river from Lambton Park to Washington Staithes. From here, 300 keels passed down river to Sunderland each tide, to load up sea-going colliers. In 1805, industrial history was made when the first

fixed engines to haul coals up an incline were introduced on the waggonway from Birtley to Black Fell, Oxclose and Washington Staithes. Coal-mining was one of Washington's oldest industries. It was first worked on Washington Moor as early as 1356 and it was here in 1718 that Thomas Newcomen built the first steam engine for draining coal mines. A ruined wall which was part of the engine-house still stands in a farm hedge.

Fatfield miners and their wives and children walk down the waggonway to the staithes during a strike in 1908, literally drumming up support in their fight for better conditions.

Washington miners scrabble for coal from the pit heap during one of the frequent strikes for improved pay and conditions or often, to try to stop the owners imposing cuts in pay or worse conditions. The picture was taken on 6 June 1921.

Harraton miners are pictured ready to go underground on 9 September 1904. Cloth caps were the norm in the days before safety helmets.

A Harraton miner pushes a pram towards the pit. The pram is more likely to have been for ferrying coals home from the pit heap than for carrying a baby.

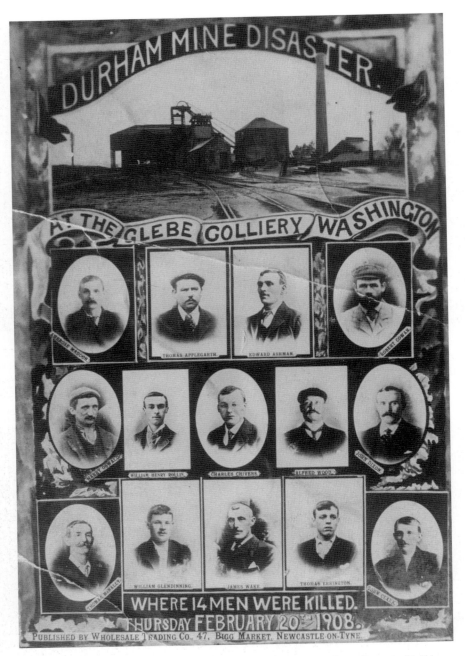

A postcard was produced in 1908 to commemorate the disaster at Glebe Colliery on 20 February. Fourteen miners were crushed and burnt to death in an explosion and one man was seriously injured. The dead were Ambrose Maddon, Thomas Applegarth, Edward Ashman, Robert Cowan, Harry Oswald, William Henry Rollin, Charles Chives, Alfred Wood, James Dixon, Thomas McNally, William Glendinning, James Wake, Thomas Herrington and John Clark. Throughout the twentieth century, mining remained the most hazardous occupations. When disaster struck, commemorative postcards like this one were produced, often to raise funds for the bereaved families.

Above and below: Funeral processions for the men killed in the Glebe Colliery disaster of February 1908. From villages throughout the Durham and Northumberland coalfield, thousands travelled by special trains, on waggons and on foot to Washington. It was estimated that more than 21,000 people arrived to pay their last respects. Mining communities were united in grief whenever a disaster occurred, families knowing all too well the dangers their own loved ones faced every day of their working lives.

Above: The winding house and headgear of Glebe Colliery with the offices to the right and store behind. This panorama was captured from Home View, The Avenue, in the mid-1960s.

Below: A close-up of Washington Glebe pit. Left of centre is the chute for loading lorries and left to right, the gantry to take tubs from ground level to the screen building. Huge quantities of pit props were stored in the pit yard, some of which can be seen to the right of the picture.

Above and below: One of the last pictures to be taken of Glebe Colliery before closure, above, and below, demolition is under way in 1973, bringing the end of an era.

Left: John George Nicholson, left, and Henry Smith were both putters at Washington F pit. Their job was to shift tubs full of coal from the face and keep the face workers supplied with empty tubs for refilling.

Below: North Biddick Colliery, which opened before 1710 and closed in 1935. This picture was taken in 1931 towards the end of its working life. The offices to the left were converted into a house, demolished in the 1970s. The loaded waggons were raised to the level of the railway line by an engine in the colliery yard.

Above: This picture of a miner riding a horse underground at Washington F pit was taken as part of a National Coal Board safety campaign. Horses and ponies were used in the local pits well after the Second World War.

Below: Colliery blacksmiths at work in Washington. Their skills were needed to keep heavy metal equipment above and below ground in working order.

These men were members of the Washington F pit rescue team in a picture taken at a social function in 1922. There was never a shortage of volunteers to help in rescues underground and despite the dangers they always carried on to the bitter end. The rescuers in the Glebe disaster were driven back six times by the fires caused by the explosion.

These men were from the last shift at Washington F pit which closed in 1968 after a working life stretching back almost 200 years. Four years before closure it was producing record tonnages.

The Washington F pit banner is paraded through packed streets on the way to the annual Durham Miners' Gala on the Racecourse in Durham City in 1936.

Usworth Colliery with the Frederick shaft in the foreground and the Victory behind. The Frederick was the coal shaft and the Victory the man-riding shaft. The low buildings on the right are the training shop and the blacksmiths' shop. The building in the left foreground is the old winding house.

The level crossing at Springwell Colliery with the Bowes Railway in the left foreground. The railway is preserved as part of the area's heritage and trains operate on special open days.

Springwell miners pose in front of their banner, depicting the Durham Miners' Association headquarters at Redhill. The picture was taken on the Racecourse at Durham during the 1923 Miners' Gala. Note how formally the miners and their families are dressed for the Big Meeting which was the highlight of their year.

Usworth miners parade their banner with the band behind over Elvet Bridge in Durham City on their way to the 1950 Big Meeting on the Racecourse. Until cars became more common, this was the one day in the year that mining families, split up as new pits opened in other parts of the coalfield, were reunited.

The last shift at Usworth, the last of the working pits in Washington. It closed in August 1974.

six

People and Places

Left: The opening of the Coxgreen footbridge over the River Wear attracted the crowds in 1958. The bridge gives easy access to walks along the banks to the Sir James Steel Park on the riverside.

Below: Fatfield Bridge was opened by the Earl of Durham in January 1891 to carry the main road from Washington to Houghton le Spring. This view from Worm Hill shows the neat rows of terraced houses and just over the bridge, the local cinema, which opened as North Biddick Miners' Hall in 1909. It was converted into the Gem Theatre and after the Second World War, changed its name to the Victory Cinema. Worm Hill, incidentally, is so named because legend has it that it was the resting place of the local dragon, the Lambton Worm, which, according to the folk song, ate livestock and bairns, and milked a dozen cows a night, until Lord Lambton's son returned from the Crusades to slay it. Most Wearsiders know the chorus: 'Whist, lads, haad your gobs/ Aa'll tell ye aal an aaful story/ Whist, lads, haad your gobs/ An' Aa'll tell ye aboot the Worm...'

Above: Styled on the Roman bridge at Alcantara in Spain, the Victoria Viaduct was named in honour of Queen Victoria on whose Coronation Day it was opened in 1838. It carried the main rail line between London and Edinburgh. The London and North Eastern Railway locomotive 4472, also known as *The Flying Scotsman*, is pictured crossing the bridge in the late 1960s.

Below: No longer in use, the Victoria Bridge still stands in all its simple grandeur, overlooking the river with its pleasant footpaths on both banks.

This page: The Rutter family seem to have had a thing about being photographed with wheels. Above left, in 1904, is William Rutter with two-year-old James George outside Bell's the plumbers, in Monument Terrace, Station Road, Usworth, while below, the family line up in Brady Square with another youngster astride a bicycle. On the right, above, in a professional portrait in Joseph Elliott's photographic studio in New Washington, we have what is believed to be a member of the Rutter family posing as a music hall act.

Above: This elaborately-dressed horse from the Co-operative Society in Spout Lane won first prize, as the label states, in the annual horse parade..

Below: Mr R.W. Greenwell, of West Mere House, Springwell, is standing beside his 1911 Albion lorry near the post office in Springwell. He operated a carrying business, ferrying parcels from Newcastle to shops in Washington. Here, however, he is believed to be giving First World War soldiers an outing in 1914.

Above: The driver adopts a casual stance in his wellington boots outside a vehicle belonging to the Northern Industrial Improvement Trust Ltd. This was formed in 1929 by the Kellett family who operated Washington collieries from the 1930s until the nationalisation of the coal industry. The Trust's registered office was Usworth Hall, New Washington, telephone Washington 61. The picture was taken in 1935 at the height of the Depression.

Below: A pre-war travelling shop operated by A. Bell, the family butcher with several shops in the colliery villages. The van advertises daily deliveries of orders.

Above: Mr Thornton and three children pose in front of one of the first buses to travel from the Washingtons to Heworth, where they met the trams. (Today, buses travel from Washington to Heworth to meet the Metro trains.) The bus above is pictured standing outside New Rows Primitive Methodist Chapel at the junction of Heworth Road and Victoria Road, New Washington.

Below: A Northern Daimler B-type bus, with driver and conductor, taken in The Avenue, Washington Village. This service operated between 1914 and 1930.

Only forty years ago, horse-drawn milk carts were still common. This one is pictured on a housing estate in Washington Village around 1965. Note the boy on the right with his enamel can.

Greta (proper name, Marguerita) Smith, née Spoors, is sitting on the running board of her father's car, a 14-horsepower Swift, in around 1930. Greta was the aunt of David Young, from whose family album the photograph is taken.

These First World War volunteers from Washington were sent to join the Green Howards at Richmond in Yorkshire in 1914 because the local regiment, the Durham Light Infantry, had a surfeit of volunteers at the time. They are training with mock rifles.

This is the Washington Home Guard on parade during the Second World War. Many of the men were in reserved occupations and did their Home Guard duty after long shifts in the pits, chemical works or one of the other heavy industries of the area.

BEST WISHES from
USWORTH CAMP.

Above left: A First World War postcard 'from your soldier boy' at Usworth Army Training Camp – better known as a World War Two RAF base, and home to 607 Squadron. The base played a crucial role in dispatching fighter aircraft to repel the Luftwaffe bombers for whom Wearside's heavy industry was a prime target. Washington also had a full-time Army camp at Black Fell.

Above right: Emily Rodham, later Mrs Forte, adopts the familiar pose of the Statue of Liberty holding her torch of freedom aloft. The picture was taken at Washington Old Hall at the end of a parade for War Weapons Week in 1940. This was the first of many fund-raising weeks held during the war years.

Below: Victory at last and up go the trestle tables in the shadow of the pithead at Usworth Colliery for a VE Day party in May 1945.

Above: Put out more flags! Organisers of the VE Day street party in Middlefield Row, near the chemical works, take a breather between games and serving teas.

Below: The tables groan with home-made cakes at this Coronation tea party for the ladies of Harraton Village in June 1953. The portrait of the Queen became a permanent feature at the community centre.

Above and below: Edwardian Christians pose in their Sunday best beside the Church Army's mobile recruitment waggon, above, while below, thirty years on, the message is the same: 'The Wages of Sin Is Death. But The Gift of God is Eternal Life. Him That Cometh unto Me I Will in No Wise Cast Out'. And above the canopy in the older photograph is emblazoned: 'God Is Love'. It looks like the same waggon in the between-the-wars picture, but the lettering has been re-done and is not so neat and clear. The horse-drawn waggon toured round the colliery villages, aiming to take the Church to the people who would not go to a church.

Above: This is New Washington Primitive Methodist church. Both Wesleyans and the breakaway 'Prims' had a strong following in the mining communities and their teaching, particularly the principles of self-help and justice, inspired many of the early leaders of the miners' union and their recruits.

Below: Portobello Methodist church was typical of many of the nineteenth-century chapels in its small size and simplicity of design, intended to foster democracy and help all members of the congregation play an equal part. The Portobello Chapel opposite Penshaw View and Cushy Cow Row survived into the 1960s but was demolished to make way for the Washington Motorway Services on the A1.

Here are three views of the staff at Usworth House in Victorian times — above left, outside what is probably the kitchen door or the door to their quarters; above right, on duty at the imposing grand entrance, and below, in the grounds (presumably the young man in straw hat lounging on the lawn in the background is a visitor). Usworth House was built by William Peareth, Clerk of the Chamber and Alderman of Newcastle, in about 1750, on land to the west of Great Usworth which he bought from one of the Hiltons. The latter were a prominent local landowning dynasty that, a few centuries earlier, had married into the Washington family and who owned Hylton Castle, to the east. Usworth House, which had a frontage of seven bays with the central three projected, was generally known as Peareth Hall. By the time of these photographs in the late nineteenth century, it was the home of John Bailey, wine merchant. It was demolished some time between 1895 and 1919, leaving just one wing intact.

Above: Staff at Usworth Station await the arrival of a train. Both passenger and freight trains (mainly carrying coal, of course) kept the station busy, while nearby Washington Station was an important rail junction. Here the Newcastle to Leamside line, via the Victoria Bridge, crossed the Stanhope to Tyne line, the latter being used to transport iron ore to the steelworks at Consett. Passenger services were withdrawn from 1963 and freight ceased in 1991. Proposals later in the 1990s to reopen the Durham to Newcastle line via Washington came to naught. Oddly enough, the announcement that the Washington to Newcastle line was to be the first to close under the Beeching Plan for the reorganisation of the railways came in the same week (July 1964) that Washington was designated a New Town. Great planning!

Below: The colliery villages were best known for their brass and silver bands, but other instruments were popular too. The harmonica players were members of Billy Bankhead's Blue Bird Band. Back row, left to right: Jack Ainsley, Jimmy Calvert, Eddie Foster and Tom Whitfield. Front row: Sid Foster, Billy Bankhead, Junior, Billy Bankhead, Senior, Billy Bohill and Jimmy McLindon.

Most local workplaces fielded their own football teams. This is Havannah Rovers, the team from Parson's engineering works, with trophies and medals won during the 1911/12 season. The picture of the team and their coaches and managers was taken in 1912. Note that the players are posing in their team places: five forwards, three half-backs, two full backs and the goalkeeper – the standard formation until the latter years of the twentieth century.

Football teams flourished in churches and chapels. The Washington United AFC team, pictured above in 1914, was based at the Wesleyan Chapel in Engine Square, beside the F pit up-cast shaft, in Windlass Lane, Albany. This team won the Washington and District League and the Washington Aged Miners' Cup in the 1913/14 season.

Colliery welfare organisations run by the miners themselves provided sports fields and often tennis courts in the pit villages. They also fielded teams in local leagues. Above is the Washington Colliery cricket team in 1935. George Muncaster, a Deputy at Washington F pit, is standing second from left and his brother Thomas is seated far left. A decade or so earlier, the Muncasters were key players in the football team, William as goalkeeper and Thomas as outside right.

Colliery welfare teams continued to flourish after the Second World War (and nationalisation of their workplaces) and were still operating when the last pits closed at the end of the twentieth century. Here we have the highly successful Washington Colliery football team and their officials, celebrating the successes of the 1954/55 season, when they won the Washington Cup, Durham Cup and local League Cup.

This is the area of old Fatfield village formerly known as The Glen. The picture was taken looking north up Biddick Lane, which is climbing towards the horizon, with Bonemill Lane on the left and Fatfield Square in the left foreground. None of the buildings in this early twentieth-century picture has survived. The area on the left was occupied by Fatfield Primary School and there is now a road junction where the two old lanes meet in the foreground. Villagers here were among the most vociferous opponents to the New Town plan of Washington Development Corporation which saw the demolition of houses to make way for roads, as well as some welcome demolition of sub-standard houses.

A reminder of the predominantly rural nature of the area comes in this pre-1900 photograph of the view looking westwards along Station Road, with the Red House on the left. Glebe Schools, later John F. Kennedy Primary, were built on the field on the right.

Girdle Cake Cottage was a popular destination for boat trips on the river. Many a Sunday School treat and family trip ended up here for afternoon tea and, yes, girdle cakes were a speciality of the house. Those requiring stronger refreshment could take the ferry across from here to the Bird in the Bush public house. The cottage was on the north bank of the river, downstream from Fatfield Bridge. The last resident was Tom Davison, a miner and fiddler, and the cottage was demolished in 1932.

New Washington fire brigade was based at the fire station behind the Bird Inn. These firemen in front of one of the fire engines were pictured in 1950. The front row includes G. Ranson, G. Longworth, T.H. Potter, and T. Hutchinson, and the back row includes Messrs Longworth, McGee and Hall.

This is a fancy dress football match organised to raise funds during a strike in the 1920s. The big strikes of 1926, and later in the century in the 1970s and 1984–85, are those that are remembered today, but in the days before nationalisation there were many smaller isolated strikes when negotiations with coal companies failed. In the 1920s, in particular, the strikes were not a bid for pay rises, but to stop pay cuts and increased hours.

Homemade entertainment and dressing up was popular among church and chapel folk. This set of gypsies is made up of ladies from the Station Road Chapel Women's Own Concert Party, which would perform for other chapels and organisations in the area.

St Cuthbert's Mission set up this soup kitchen, serving hot broth, bread, and cocoa to alleviate hardship during the First World War. Local miners suffered from cuts in both rates of pay and hours of work as well as facing wartime price rises – they could not afford to feed their families. In 1917, children at nine Washington schools went on strike to draw attention to the plight of 1,600 miners in Usworth and Washington, where their fathers had had their shifts cut to less than half and pay was down to 26s or even lower. Within two days, the children won – Durham County Council adjusted regulations for relief, so that no family should have less than £2 1s a week.

A funeral procession around the time of the First World War makes its solemn progress through Washington Station. Note the elaborate horse-drawn cortége laden with flowers and the wreaths being carried by two of the women mourners. Most mining families paid weekly insurance policies to guarantee they had the money for a decent funeral.

The close bond forged underground carried on in the social life of miners, with workmates enjoying one another's company. The provenance of this picture is not known but it is a typical pre-Second World War off-duty gathering, with cloth caps and watch chains de rigueur. The front row includes Messrs Dodds, Richardson, Conroy and Hughes, and further back are Messrs Bell, Oliver, Ross and Whitfield.

Community action in progress during the 1968 Clean Up Washington drive. In shirt sleeves in the centre is Mr Stephen Holley, General Manager of Washington Development Corporation, with to the right the Corporation's chairman, Sir James Steel, both of them lending a helping hand to Mr Geoff Judson, a member of the congregation, and members of the youth group, in clearing land belonging to Washington parish church. The greening of Washington was a key priority of the Development Corporation in seeking to make the New Town attractive to new industry and new residents.

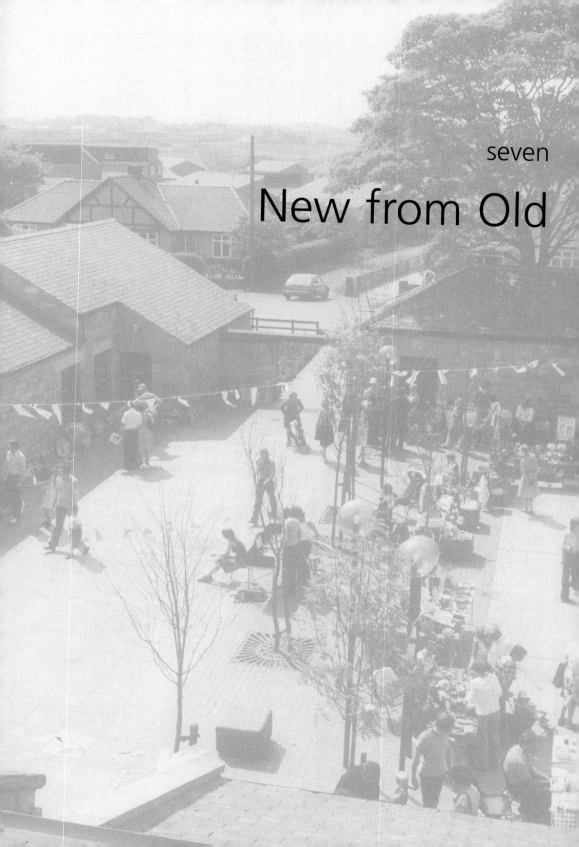

seven

New from Old

Above and below: No, these pictures have not escaped from the industry section of this book! They are all examples of the past being preserved for present and future enjoyment. Above, a replica of the famous Sans Pareil engine gets up steam at the preserved Bowes Railway at Springell and below, a sturdy carthorse pulls chaldron waggons at a Railway Pioneers event. Activities during the railway's open days and weekends are popular with all the family. Even in 2006, a ride on a steam train is a treat that is hard to beat.

Right and below: The last coal was drawn from Washington F pit on June 21, 1968. The National Coal Board presented the winding house and headgear to the people of Washington to mark the importance of mining in the area, and the site in Albany Way was opened as a museum in 1976. It closed as a cost-cutting measure in 2000, but remains intact – as these views of the exterior and the automatic expansion gear inside demonstrate – and is currently open to the public

on certain weekends of the year. The site's mining history dates from 1775 when Robert Shafto, Sir Gilfrid Lawson and Dr James Musgrave, lords of the manor of Washington, leased land to Sunderland coal-fitter William Russell, who sank a series of pits, each known by a letter of the alphabet from A to I in the area that became New Washington. The first coals were drawn in March 1778. The F pit, originally sunk in 1777, was remodelled for the third and last time in 1903, and this is when the great winding engine, built in 1888, was bought second-hand, though no one knows where it came from. In 1927, electricity was introduced. The engine could lift 120 tons of coal an hour to the surface. In 1953-54 the shaft was deepened to reach the Busty seam, 929ft down. The pit reached its peak in 1964-5, with 1,500 men producing 486,000 tons of coal a year. It did not fit 'super pit' policy and closed three years later. Demonstrations and guided tours are given during open days, when children's activities are also organised.

Washington Wildfowl and Wetlands Centre opened in 1975 on former farmland and on the site of the old Barmston Forge, run by a family of metalworkers and keel-builders in the nineteenth century. The wildfowl refuge was the idea of Sir James Steel, chairman of Washington Development Corporation, which acquired the land and created the centre to a design provided by world-famous naturalist Sir Peter Scott, honorary director of the Wildfowl Trust. The Prince of Wales is pictured between Sir Peter and Sir James on a visit to the centre in 1983, with the then curator, Brian Gadsby, crouching to feed some Hawaiian geese, which breed at the Centre. The birds, found in abundance when Captain Cook arrived in Hawaii, had been reduced to only thirty when Sir Peter was alerted to the danger of extinction. He brought the first pair of Hawaiian geese to Britain in 1950. Now families of Hawaiian geese are a favourite attraction at Washington and the other six refuges he created in Britain.

Left: Local schoolchildren are pictured identifying birds and their habitat in 1992. Within two years of opening, 150 species of birds had been recorded at the refuge and over the years, more hides have been created for viewing. Education was an important part of the Centre's work from the beginning and an education extension was opened by Sir Peter Scott in 1986. A wetland discovery centre was officially opened by Professor David Bellamy and Dr Joe Baker in 1996 and an early years play area was added to the Centre's attractions in 2003 to increase the enjoyment of the youngest visitors.

The Duchess of Gloucester admires young mute swans and a Hawaiian goose on a 1980 visit to Washington Wetlands Centre, escorted by Sir James Steel as Lord Lieutenant, far right. Water for the Centre is recycled from the sewage treatment works established nearby by Washington Development Corporation. Further ponds were excavated in 1980 and two reservoirs combined into one large water body in 1994. In 2005, work began on two new wetland creation projects. Chris Francis, centre manager since 1991, says the emphasis in recent years has shifted towards that of nature reserve. The trees planted thirty years ago now encourage woodland flowers and birds. A reed bed is being created to attract more insects and wetland flowers. Dragonflies and butterflies, water voles, marsh orchids, forget-me-nots and birdsfoot trefoil are all part of the rich pattern of nature to be found here - though they may find it hard to compete for attention with special events like the hatching of avocet chicks this year.

Above and below: A refuge for all seasons, as these pictures show. Above, the popular sitting-out area in the 1980s, with the original visitor centre behind. Work on an extension began in 1994 and a new café opened the following year, again with tables and chairs outside to enjoy summer weather. The Centre is open every day except Christmas Day and attracts visitors even on cold winter days, though probably not in February 1979, when conservation staff were pictured clearing snow to feed the birds and found that as soon as they broke through the ice to the water, it froze over again.

In 1980, wildfowl in the Wetlands Centre enjoyed this fine view of Penshaw Monument on the horizon. The Victorian folly modelled on the Temple of Theseion in Athens was built in honour of John George ('Radical Jack') Lambton, a leader of the campaign for parliamentary reform in 1832. He was author of the Durham Report on Canada which was the foundation document of the Commonwealth of Nations and was a popular local coal-owner. As early as the 1820s, he allowed membership of the miners' union and contributed to accident insurance and a rudimentary pension scheme for men in his pits. A procession of 50,000 people followed his coffin on the day of his funeral in 1840. Now, his monument, a landmark for miles around, is glimpsed less clearly at the Wetlands Centre as the trees planted thirty years ago have grown to provide pleasant woodland.

Left and below: A view through the arches of the byres to the granary at the old North Biddick Farm around forty years ago (below) shows the amount of work needed to convert it to a thriving arts centre. The conversion and restoration retained the charm of the original architecture and most of the stonework, and the arts centre was opened in 1977 by Sir James Steel, chairman of Washington Development Corporation. The restored granary building is shown left and further views of the converted byres and cowsheds are on the following pages. The main buildings were converted into the Granary bar/restaurant, the High Barn Theatre, and a large art gallery and reception area, while the old stables, byres and cowsheds became offices, craft workshops, community space, arts workshop and practice room for the Washington Music Co-operative. The centre is a popular venue for live music, including regular folk and rock nights.

The byres and other old outbuildings of North Biddick Farm became showcases and workplaces for local craftsmen. Early residents included Barry Oliver, a violin-maker, below, and Alan Ball, a potter, pictured above putting pots in his kiln, and with a display of finished pots in the window. Note how the old arches have been retained.

The old and the new. The converted outbuildings of North Biddick Farm surround a courtyard, once the old farmyard, and beyond, new roads and housing of a pleasantly rural part of Biddick. The above picture was taken in the 1980s at one of the monthly art marts. These are still held on the first Saturday

of every month, but these days opt to use the art gallery and theatre areas indoors. The courtyard is still well used in summer, when the real-ale bar puts tables and chairs outside.

Other local titles published by Tempus

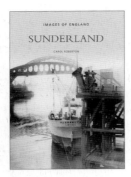

Sunderland

CAROL ROBERTON

Sunderland's appearance has changed more in the last decade than in the whole century before with barely a trace left of the great traditions of coalmining, shipbuilding and marine engineering for which the town was once famous. This fascinating book of photographs, selected mainly from the archives of the *Sunderland Echo,* recalls the busy industrial times of the last hundred years.

0 7524 3616 3

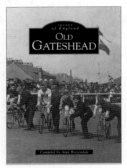

Old Gateshead

ALAN BRAZENDALE

This collection of 200 photographs of the old part of Gateshead captures the essence of the town in the late nineteenth and early twentieth centuries. This was a period of great expansion and change, during which the last vestiges of the area's rural past finally vanished and the great industries, which made the whole of Tyneside famous, reached their heyday. The pictures, many drawn from the collection held at Gateshead Library, show factories and warehouses, shops and private dwellings, schools and churches, transport and local people.

0 7524 2073 9

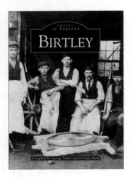

Birtley

GEORGE NAIRN AND DOROTHY RAND

This selection of old photographs comes largely from the personal archive of old picture postcards collected by the authors. Through these old images we can see the Birtley of the last century in all its variety: streets, buildings, schools, shops, churches and people at work and play. The book is an important social history of the town.

0 7524 0366 4

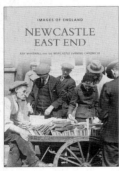

Newcastle East End

RAY MARSHALL

This book is a fascinating photographic record of the East End of Newcastle through the twentieth century. The images were selected by Ray Marshall from the *Newcastle Evening Chronicle's* archives and will provide a nostalgic tour for all who have lived or worked in this historic and now much changed area.

0 7524 3629 5

If you are interested in purchasing other books published by Tempus, or in case you have difficulty finding any Tempus books in your local bookshop, you can also place orders directly through our website

www.tempus-publishing.com